SIGNSPOTTING 3

The Five Mile Press Pty Ltd
1 Centre Road, Scoresby
Victoria 3179 Australia
www.fivemile.com.au

First published 2009

Printed in China

Page design by Salmon Design

National Library of Australia Cataloguing-in-Publication entry:

Signspotting 3 : Lost in translation / Doug Lansky.

978 1 74211 652 5 (pbk.)

Signs and signboards--Humour.

302.230207

LOST IN TRANSLATION

SIGNSPOTTING

3

Compiled by Doug Lansky

INTRODUCTION

→ It's hard to imagine a world without signs. No stop signs, no arrows, no speed limits, no warnings. No bright colours screaming for your attention. Take a good look next time you step outside – signs are virtually everywhere. In the county of Kent, England, alone (presumably the only county that bothered to count), they discovered they had 140,000 signs.

But do we really need them – any of them? In 2007, the German town of Bohmte (population 13,000) decided to remove all of their signs and street markings. They even took away the kerbs, footpaths and traffic lights. And they're paying more than 2.3 million euros to do it. Why? Because – this is true – they wanted to make their roads safer. They had tried speed traps and cross walks – the usual fixes – but those didn't seem to keep the cars and trucks from racing through their main street, treating pedestrians and cyclists like expendable supporting characters in a video game.

Taking a page out of the reverse psychology handbook, Bohmte decided drivers were too comfortable with signs – to the point that they ignored them. By removing them, they believed drivers would get nervous and hit the brakes. The roads were remade with a burnt sienna brick to give a subtle indication that drivers were entering a special zone. 'Generally speaking, what we want is for people to be confused. When they're confused, they'll be more alert and drive more carefully,' Bohmte's deputy mayor, Willi Ladner, told the *Washington Post* just as the new system opened.

Naturally, without marked spaces, people can park as they please as long as – here comes unwritten rule number one – they don't leave them in the middle of the road. The other unwritten rules are yielding to anything coming from the right (car, bus, bike or pedestrian) and sticking to the nationwide 30 kilometres per hour limit for city driving

What happened? One eyewitness, Tony Paterson, a newspaper reporter from London's *Independent*, noted that vehicles that 'pass along this stretch of sign-free road seem to be driven by swivel-headed paranoiacs with rubber vertebrae.
They crawl along at little more than 15 miles per hour [25 km/h], their occupants constantly craning their necks to make doubly sure that they are not going to hit anything, be it a pedestrian, cyclist, or even another car.'

This 'shared space' concept is the work of legendary Dutch traffic engineer Hans Monderman, who wants road users to negotiate with hand signals and eye contact instead of traffic signs. ('If you treat people like idiots, they'll act like idiots,' he likes to say.) In the Dutch town of Drachten, removing the signs not only reduced accidents, but kept traffic more fluid and reduced fuel consumption. In Haren, another recently signless Dutch town, the number of accidents at one intersection dropped by 95 per cent

Now this shared space program is being subsidised across the European Union. And interest is spreading worldwide.

Where does this leave signspotters? Don't despair ... experts believe that the shared space program works best in smaller towns (with intersections hosting less than 15,000 vehicles a day) and for just short sections of road. More than that and drivers lose patience with the concept. Besides, after paying to take away the signs, Bohmte decided to explain this new sign-free policy by – you'll never guess – putting up a sign.

→ Seems like the lifesaving aspect needs a bit of work.

Location → Pt Reyes National Seashore, California, USA
Credit → Eris Weaver

→ Take Crop Patterns 101, study advanced spacecraft sightings, and take field trips to Area 51.

Location → Tirana, Albania
Credit → James Wilson

→ Welcome to Paradise Interiors. Where we bring your decorating dreams to life.

Location → New Delhi, India
Credit → Sandra Kell

→ Just to be safe, you probably don't want to order a slushie here.

Location → Las Vegas, New Mexico, USA
Credit → Camille Potts

BY THE NUMBERS

→ **500,000,000** Native English speakers

882,000,000 Native Mandarin speakers

1.5 billion Total English speakers

24,000–30,000 Vocabulary of an educated native English speaker

3000 Words used in a 'working vocabulary'

300,000 English 'head words' in the *Oxford English Dictionary*. Not including **615,000** versions of these words

225,000 Spanish words in contemporary use

100,000 French words in contemporary use

25,525 French words recognised by the French lingual governing body, Academié Française

89 Percentage of European Union school children who study English as a foreign language

32 Percentage of European Union school children who study French as a foreign language

8 Percentage of European Union school children who study Spanish as a foreign language

87 Percentage of Dutch who speak English

51 Percentage of Germans who speak English

60 Percentage of Finns who speak English

→ Get that 'fried liver' freshness you've been missing.

Location → Joshua Tree National Park, California, USA
Credit → Bob Ecker

→ Sales have been flat lately.

Location → Bishop, California, USA
Credit → Robert Firth

MASSACHUSETTS STATE HOUSE

→ **General Hooker Entrance**

Bowdoin St. Entrance ♿

Ashburton Park Entrance ♿

→ Apparently, the specialist hookers have their own entrance.

Location → Boston, Massachusetts, USA
Credit → James Henderson

Danger
Sharp spikes
near groynes

→ C'mon, jump in! It's not like there are giant spikes in the water specially placed to spear you in the nether regions.

Location → Southwold, Suffolk, England
Credit → Daniel Swallow

→ Nice to see people taking a stand against racism – and eating outside.

Location → Shimla, India
Credit → Erika Rogers

→ Don't even think about entering.

Location → Granada, Spain
Credit → Annie Durkin

→ When a pornographer takes a day job making signs.

Location → San Francisco, California, USA
Credit → Myla Ablog

→ Welcome to the Insane Lane.

→ At least they're up-front about where the food will end up.

Location → Washington DC, USA
Credit → William Nichols

Location → Hong Kong, China
Credit → Tony HW Kee

СПАСАТЕЛЬНЫЙ ЖИЛЕТ
ПОД ВАШИМ КРЕСЛОМ
LIVE VEST UNDER YOUR SEAT
سترة النجاة تحت مقعدك

→ Don't worry, your vest has been trained to handle emergencies.

Location → Egyptian Air flight to Abu Simbel, Egypt
Credit → Judi Quan

→ Nothing like the smell of fresh Farturas first thing in the morning.

Location → Algeciras, Spain
Credit → Claire Lowry

→ Welcome All Indecisive Convention Members!

Location → Kemmerer, Wyoming, USA
Credit → Chan Weller

→ The breakfast of champions.

Location → Miami, Florida, USA
Credit → Annie Flynn

→ Two roads diverged in a wood, and I – I took the usual route.

Location → Nara, Japan
Credit → Shawn Dunning

→ If you're looking for Somass, you might try
  Vancouver Island!

Location   → Port Alberni, British Columbia, Canada
Credit   → Storm Cunningham

→ Er ... yes it is.

Location   → Stratton, England
Credit   → Paul Stevens

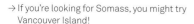

← 020   → Ah, the perks of being the Messiah.

Location   → Grand Rapids, Michigan, USA
Credit   → Melanie Redman

→ Is your fish getting a bit slimy? Seaweed between the scales? Extra fishy smell?
Maybe it's time to get your pet fish professionally washed.

Location   → Denver, Colorado, USA
Credit   → Deanna Clark

→ Your leg is missing ... SURPRISE!

Location → Key Largo, Florida, USA
Credit → Gary Vandekerckhove

→ Presumably more profitable than the Health Valley Death Center.

Location → Death Valley, California, USA
Credit → John Goldman

→ Putting those welfare cheques to good use.

Location → Welfare, Texas, USA
Credit → Tom Crawford

→ We will be checking very carefully for concealed weapons.

Location → Cairns, Australia
Credit → Kristen Norton

← 026 → It's raining men.

Location → Mertola, Portugal
Credit   → Sarah Eriksen

→ To serve and protect and commit.

Location → Pt Reyes National Seashore, California, USA
Credit   → Eris Weaver

→ If you feel something slithering around your legs, it's probably just an enormous jellyfish. Happens all the time. Enjoy the water!

Location → Cape Tribulation Beach, Queensland, Australia
Credit → Sarah Good

→ You can hardly expect drivers on LSD to stick to one lane.

Location → Georgia, USA
Credit → Tom Trocine

→ Finally, a head-smashed-in buffalo jump that's disabled-accessible and has a payphone.

Location → Trans-Canada Highway, Canada
Credit → Clair Thompson

→ British Telecom has a wicked sense of humour.

Location → Norfolk, England
Credit → Tim Bentinck

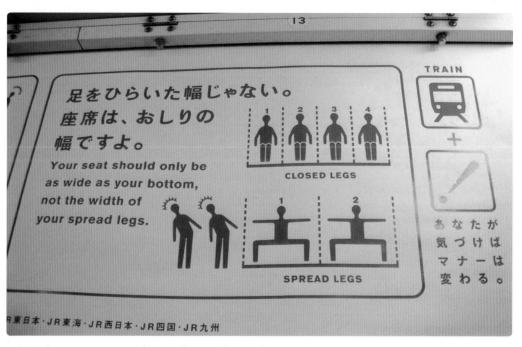

→ Evidently, sumo warm-up exercises are also out of the question.

Location → Tokyo, Japan
Credit → Tanja Sobbo

**Oldies but goldies
- meals they made in Prague
100 years ago**

**Stará dobrá klasika,
aneb co se vařilo v Praze
před 100 lety**

→ It's not easy to cut through the famous 100-year-old top layer of fungus on the soup, but otherwise it's not bad.

Location → Prague, Czech Republic
Credit → Lynn Levy

→ Marilyn Monroe crossing?

Location → Johannesburg, South Africa
Credit → Christine Ayers

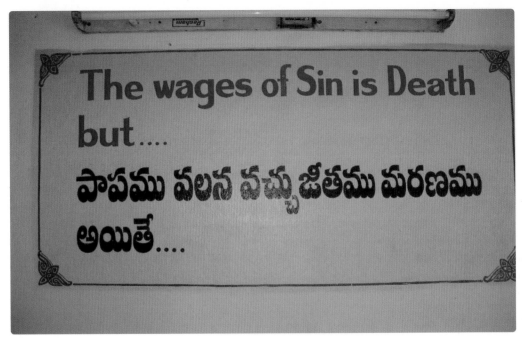

Location   → Andhra Pradesh, India
Credit   → Gary Cox

→ Suppose you should probably follow it.

Location → Trans-Canada Highway
Credit → Clair Thompson

WORDSPOTTING

→ English is growing. Not just the number of people who speak it, but the actual number of words. According to word analyst Paul JJ Payack of the Global Language Monitor, there's a new word added every 98 seconds and, for the first time in history for any language, English will have passed the one million word mark by the time this book is released.

This growth is largely due to the internationalisation of the language in all its variants (Chinglish, Fringlish, as well as Snoop Dogg's 'shizzle' rap language and George W Bush's often-quoted malapropisms such as 'misunderestimate'), as well as the popular spread of English itself. English as a global language may have been kick-started by the British Empire and then piggybacked a ride on the economic and cultural power of the United States, but it's now fuelled and distributed largely by the internet. As soon as new words are coined, they zip across the web with the help of sites like Urbandictionary.com. With more words and expressions that can be mangled and more English speakers to mangle them, the future of funny signs looks promising.

→ Sure, it's a little stuffy inside, but at least he's honest about it.

Location → Copenhagen, Denmark
Credit   → Barbara Z Moss

→ Coming soon! The first zoo employee born in captivity.

Location → Natural Bridge, Virginia, USA
Credit → Rhonda Maloney

→ Possible motto: 'Our customers aren't too picky.'

Location   → Hong Kong, China
Credit   → M Madhy

← 038   → All applicants must be at least somewhat dead.

Location   → Langley, Canada
Credit   → Maryalice Wood

Welcome to
Community School of
Excellence!!

Please repot to the
Main Office

→ Please Repot to the Kommunity Skool of Exselence!!!

Location   → St Paul, Minnesota, USA
Credit   → Donald Reeder

→ Finally, a restaurant that combines the famous taste of railway cuisine with the practicality of a stomach clinic. All for a reasonable price.

Location → Nairobi, Kenya
Credit → Tom Harm

→ Extreme urban driving: the inverted U-turn.

Location → Cottage Grove, Minnesota, USA
Credit → Larry Holmen

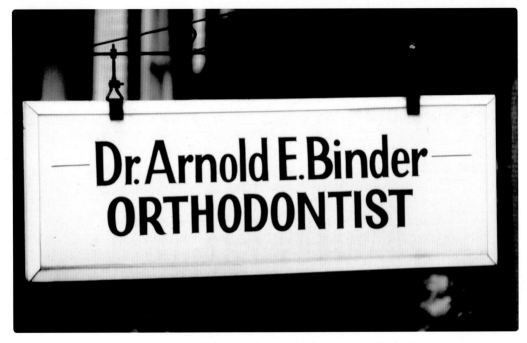

→ Career choices were limited: It was either orthodontics, prison guard in Guantanamo or dominatrix.

Location   → Littleton, Massachusetts, USA
Credit   → Jim McGrath

→ It's actually for a cooking centre. Simon Cowell only vacations here.

Location   → Montego Bay, Jamaica
Credit   → Laura Skrypchak

→ It's not always easy to tell the difference between wight and wong.

Location → South Island, New Zealand
Credit → Carol Veesaert

→ And the Academy Award for Stick Figure in a Dramatic Pose goes to ...

Location → Granville Island, Vancouver, British Columbia, Canada
Credit → Turi Henderson

→ Sorry, no toilet diving.

Location → Saudi Arabia
Credit → Fatima Alaiwat

Location → Between Hangzhou and Shanghai, China
Credit → Richard Patenaude

← 048   → Pre-internet chat room.

Location   → Chiang Mai, Thailand
Credit   → Adrian Liston

→ Protected by contractors.

Location → London, England
Credit → Nick Forester

→ For those who decide not to stop at church.

Location → Grand Cayman, Cayman Islands
Credit → Erica Pagliuco

→ Great moments in history: 'This place is just beautiful and I know exactly what I'm going to call it ...'

Location → Newfoundland, Canada
Credit → Kathleen Ninneman

→ Those customs officers can get a bit frisky.

Location → Buenos Aires, Argentina
Credit → Caroline Born

→ Welcome to bear puppet theatre!

→ Finally, a country that treats jaywalking seriously.

Location → Mt Lemmon, Arizona, USA
Credit → Nancy Corbett

Location → Kuwait City, Kuwait
Credit → Leila Mansouri

→ Looks like it may be time to change the town's name.

Location → Arkansas, USA
Credit   → Larry Shortell

→ Go on, what are you waiting for? Run into it.

→ Thank God, that bicycle was killing me.

Location → Dai Village, Southern China
Credit → Peggie Wormington

Location → Dublin, Ireland
Credit → Linda E Burg

→ 'Modern' family-planning advice.

Location   → Northampton, England
Credit   → Adena Goodart

→ Surround yourself with scores of retired Germans in motorhomes. Enjoy our community bathrooms.
We're waiting for you to visit us here in Hell.

Location → Near Fugen, Austria
Credit → Lisa Bush

→ Bowling for hoes.

Location → Kingston, New York, USA
Credit → Leanne Pearce

→ Impressive ... an entire building devoted to just one ageing body part.

Location → Auckland, New Zealand
Credit → Andrew Lister

→ Please wait for the door to turn green before opening.

Location → Glastonbury, England
Credit → Philip Scadding

← 060   → That whole 'up' and 'down' business is pretty confusing stuff.

Location   → Philadelphia, Pennsylvania, USA
Credit   → Rebecca Solomon

→ When in use, this sign will look totally different.

Location → Denbigh, Wales
Credit → Vig Smyth

→ Just don't go there.

Location → Commerce City, Colorado, USA
Credit → John McLaughlin

→ Chinese hospitality aimed at the short-term visitor.

Location → Guangzhou, China
Credit → Annette Sorenson

~ 喫煙されるお客様へ ~
構内は禁煙になっております、
外の喫煙コーナーでお願いします。

Building asks a smoked visitor
in the outside smoking section
that you cannot smoke in.

→ In short, 'No Smoking'.

Location → Hakone, Japan
Credit → Frank McLarnon

→ Just in case you were thinking of walking up to that cement precipice and taking a photo.

Location   → Shennong Stream, China
Credit   → Andrew Fogg

お願い

この洗面台では、髪を洗ったり
洗濯等をしないで下さい。

NOTICE

No washing hair or clothes
in the toilet please.

→ You know us tourists, always jamming our heads into the toilet or using the water to wash our clothes.

Location → Shinjuku, Tokyo, Japan
Credit   → Kasper Hemmer Pihl

→ There's a special on half-eaten hamburgers.

Location → Luxembourg, Belgium
Credit → Young S Ham

→ Oddly, porn rentals are down this month.

Location → Farmington, New Mexico, USA
Credit → Carolyn Fox

→ Crossing for those with jeans is up ahead.

Location → Al Udeid, Qatar
Credit → Rick Kuehn

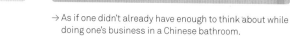

温馨提示
为避免水溅出
请您拉上浴帘

The Sweet Hint
In order not to the water splashes
please pull up the bath curtain

小心地滑

Be careful! Landslide

→ As if one didn't already have enough to think about while
doing one's business in a Chinese bathroom.

Location → Bathroom in the Redwall Hotel, Beijing, China
Credit → Henrik Hanson

皇帝净房基址

The former address of the emperor's toilet

→ The other crown jewels.

Location → Imperial Palace, Chengde, China
Credit → Sharon Oppegard

DO NOT

BEND, BORROW, BREAK, CUT, CLEAVE, CLIP, CRUSH,
DIVIDE, ENDANGER, HARM, MUTILATE, PARE, PINCH,
PICK, PLUCK, PULL, SEVER, SNIP, SNAP OFF, STEAL,
TAKE, TOUCH, TWIST OFF OR REMOVE

THE FLOWERS AND PLANTS

BY ORDER
RESIDENT ADMINISTRATOR

→ Try to find a loophole in this horticultural directive.

Location → Pune, India
Credit → Akash Shah

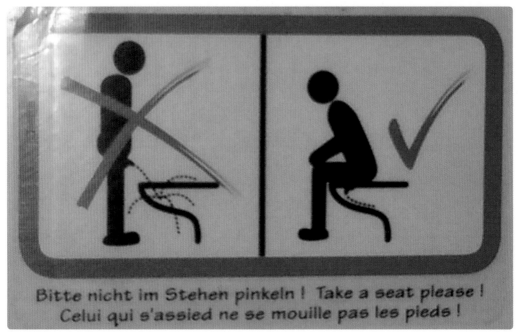

Bitte nicht im Stehen pinkeln ! Take a seat please !
Celui qui s'assied ne se mouille pas les pieds !

→ Women of the world unite!

Location → Ski lodge, Switzerland
Credit → Abbey Cape

→ Is it dancing they don't want, or that specific disco move where you point to the ceiling?

Location   → Rome, Italy
Credit   → Sofia Willner

→ 'Hey, Mum, look how close to the edge I can get!'

Location → Cliffs of Moher, Ireland
Credit → Peter Heelan

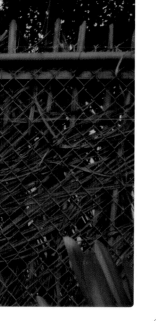

→ Cannibal or pregnant lady? Either way ...

Location → Punta Cana Resort, Dominican Republic
Credit → Alexandra Darke

→ Beware of break-dancing!

Location → Pisa, Italy (inside the Leaning Tower of Pisa)
Credit → Philip Koopman

→ Most of us thought this had been banned, at least in public.

Location → St Helens, Merseyside, England
Credit → Ray Bishop

→ Not sure if this is a bath you'd want to take.

Location   → Bangalore, India
Credit   → Rohan Bhagwat

→ Finally, a transgender bathroom.

Location → Nantong, China
Credit → Ole Rud Hansen

保护文物

HELP PROTECT THE CULTURAL RELICS

爱护栏杆

HELP PROTECT THE RAILINGS

中国人寿 敬赠
CHINA LIFE

→ Please help us save these priceless thousand-year-old relics and also this cheap stainless-steel railing.

Location → Beijing, China
Credit → Paul Bolding

→ Number 1 costs 2 and number 2 costs 3. Or, as it's also known, pay-per-poo premium.

Location → Pokhara, Nepal
Credit → Dianne Sharma-Winter

WORDSPOTTING

→ Signs may not be disappearing anytime soon, but some of the funniest ones are.

English-speaking countries are cracking down on bad signage. A new multi-billion-dollar airport terminal can expect to spend more than $10 million on signage and $1.5 million on signage consulting fees. These sign consultants or 'wayfinders' like David Roberts of Carter & Burgess Inc face more issues than you might think. Aside from clearing up confusing directions to gates and luggage carousels (or lack thereof), they need to figure out whether signs should be multilingual, and if so, which language should come first. Then there are the competing interests: the airport executives want clear signage that maximises passenger flow; the airport maintenance crew wants easy-care signs (that is, no light bulbs or extra pieces); the airport architects want signs that don't detract from their design; the airport lawyers want signs that avoid liability; and, on top of that, the wayfinders like David Roberts want consistency. There shouldn't be, for example, one restroom with 'bathroom' on the door and another with the word 'toilet'. Suddenly it doesn't seem like such a cushy job.

For the signs that have been 'fixed' already, this series of Signspotting books may become a historical reference. For those signs that aren't yet extinct, these books represent an endangered species list of sorts. But until every city, town, highway, shopping mall and retail shop starts employing wayfinders and setting up hotlines, it's fair to assume we can count on many more years of entertainment with new puzzling signs going up every day.

→ Just to make things a little more difficult.

Location → Canal in the United Kingdom
Credit → Russell Greig

→ Take away all the tailgate slamming and vibrators and what else is there to do?

Location   → Oak Creek, Wisconsin, USA
Credit   → Ron Clone

→ Meet the first stick-figure porn star.

Location → Singapore
Credit → Daniel Goldsmith

→ The self-serve buffet breakfast is better known as the Ufuk Yourself.

Location   → Istanbul, Turkey
Credit   → Peter Wilkins

→ You don't want to piss off 'Mom'.

Location → Chiang Mai, Thailand
Credit → Kelly Dyer

FREEZING GASES &
SMALL OBJECTS
MAY BE
DISCHARGED
WITHOUT NOTICE.
STAY BACK 20 FEET!

→ This would be a fun sign to have on the refrigerator.

Location → San Francisco, California, USA
Credit → Jeanine Alexander

留待他人共养眼

Please do not catch the crabs

게가 모로 가는것은 기이하므로
타인의 관상용으로 남겨주십시오

カニが横行するのは奇想だ

→ STDs respond well to politeness.

Location → Wudang Shan, China
Credit   → Per-Olof Seiron

→ Not a bad sign for a mechanic in Germany, but this sign is in California.

Location → San Mateo, California, USA
Credit → Leo Duerr

→ I'd like that 'Hey asshole!' style you had featured last week.

Location → Elmina, Ghana
Credit → Emily Osborne

THIS TOILET IS FITTED WITH

AN ELECTRONIC SHREDDING DEVICE.

PLEASE DO NOT

PUT OR FLUSH SANITARY TOWLELS, TAMPONS, HARD ARTICALS, COTTON, CONDOMS, OR PLASTIC DOWN THE TOILET.

PLEASE USE THE BIN PROVIDED

FOR THESE ITEMS.

THANK YOU FOR YOUR CO-OPERATION.

→ Introducing: a toilet for thrill seekers.

Location → St Andrews, Scotland
Credit → Laura Adrian

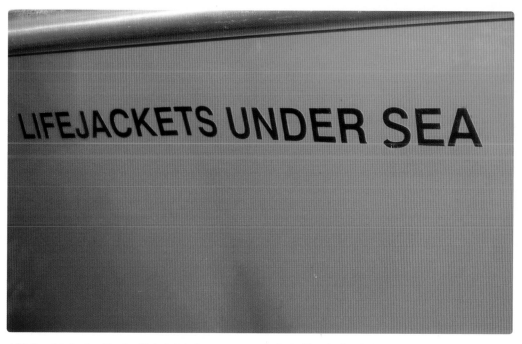

→ We thought about putting the life jackets in the rooms or maybe in the life rafts, but there was more space in the sea.

Location   → A lifeboat on the *Holland America Westerdam*
Credit   → Anne Oulahan

→ Daily Dung – get it while it's warm!

Location → Ho Chi Minh City, Vietnam
Credit → Maryalice Wood

विमानपत्तन नियंत्रक
AIRPORT CONTROLLER

अति विशिष्ट मेहमान कक्ष
V. I. P. ROOM

→ Very Immense Person Room. Your legs must be at least three metres long.

Location → Varanasi, India
Credit → Daniel Goldsmith

→ World food shortage inspires new themed deli.

Location → New York City, New York, USA
Credit → Sondra Harris

→ One man's pet is another man's meal.

Location → Chicago, Illinois, USA
Credit → Elizabeth Winkowski

→ Citizens to the left, foreign nationals and intergalactic visitors to the right.

Location → Border between Thailand and Cambodia, Poipet, Cambodia
Credit → Sanne Heine

海底椰木瓜炖雪蛤膏　￥36

Braised papaya and ovary of wild frog
Айва вала кокоса seabed китайская
flowering варит астир clam снежка

→ Even the French have a hard time swallowing this one.

Location → China
Credit → Lesley Mitchell

→ Hey Dad, the weirdest thing happened. I was at this school event and my report card got burned.

Location → Sudbury, Massachusetts, USA
Credit → Jim McGrath

→ Dr Latex and Dr Coldfingers are also available.

Location   → Melbourne, Florida, USA
Credit   → Maxwell Brown

→ Let's discuss the price outside.

Location → Eastern USA
Credit → Jeff Ference

→ Help! The keg is nearly empty!

Location → Dominican Republic
Credit → Alle Hurst

→ For plants trying to kick their petrochemical dependence.

→ Finally, the moron is here.

Location → La Jolla, California, USA
Credit → Shannon Kelley

Location → Beaune, France
Credit → Andrew Lister

→ Sending customers 'home' with love.

Location → Somanya, Ghana
Credit → Penny Pitterson

TRAFO - 2

PLEASE **NOTHING IN TOILET**
YOU CAN'T EAT   FLUSH

→ Presumably topless urination is common in this part of Croatia.

Location → Split, Croatia
Credit → Caitlin Thomas

→ That's setting the standards a bit high.

Location → Boat to Great Barrier Reef, Australia
Credit → Jean Simat

→ Just throw it in the water.

Location → Puerto San José, Guatemala
Credit → Kim Haney

→ Even after leaving office, the former president is still contributing to greenhouse emissions.

Location → Slinger, Wisconsin, USA
Credit → Marina Vobroucek

→ One small victory: Path 1, hiker 0.

Location → Stenhousemuir, Central Scotland
Credit → Stuart Craw

reserved seating area
for customers with
special needs and
unaccompanied minors

→ Going that extra mile to pamper and tend to passengers.

Location → Heathrow Airport – BMI Gateway, England
Credit → John M Silverberg

→ Shake those tenderloins.

Location → Star Valley, Arizona, USA
Credit → Susan Mann

→ What, no yak pizza?

Location → Manang, Nepal
Credit → William Bakker

→ Who knew you could find irony in a parking lot?

Location → Brookfield, Wisconsin, USA
Credit → Sarah Hoffman

→ Of course, God will smite you if you try to interpret this in an impure way.

Location → McCandless, Pennsylvania, USA
Credit → Donna Beer Stolz

→ How long is it?

Location → Ho Chi Minh City, Vietnam
Credit → Mike Blomgren

→ Maybe it's an ad for a nasal spray.

Location → Rome, Oregon, USA
Credit → Ellen Findlay Herdegen

← 114   → In some countries it's okay to put up a sign about it.

Location   → Ho Chi Minh City, Vietnam
Credit   → Mike Blomgren

TAXI Waiting Point
(No Waiting)

的士等候處

(不准停車等候)

→ You might consider the bus.

Location   → Hong Kong
Credit   → Erik Widmark

→ Watch out for car-eating cows.

Location → Western Australia
Credit → Erik Graafland

→ You never know when it's going to strike.

Location   → Vienna, Austria
Credit   → Barb Burchill

→ When 'Beware of Dogs' doesn't provide quite
  enough security.

Location   → Maui, Hawaii, USA
Credit   → Barb Burchill

→ Not-so-scenic overlook.

Location → Hoover Dam, Nevada, USA
Credit → John Daniels

→ No swimming allowed if you are a freakish fishman alien.

Location → Plitvice Lakes National Park, Croatia
Credit → Andy Baltes

→ You never know when a body bag might come in handy.

Location → Department store in Florence, Italy
Credit → Katie Abbott

→ Coconuts are getting organised and they know what they want.

Location → Haarlem, Netherlands
Credit → John Mackessack

→ Try the new recreational cemetery: it's loads of fun. Great for the whole family.

Location → Rice Lake, Wisconsin, USA
Credit → James Slauson

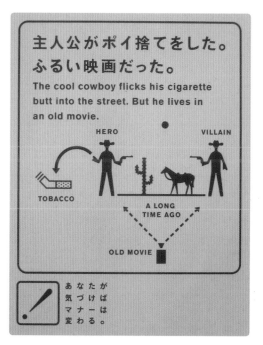

主人公がポイ捨てをした。
ふるい映画だった。

The cool cowboy flicks his cigarette
butt into the street. But he lives in
an old movie.

HERO

VILLAIN

TOBACCO

A LONG
TIME AGO

OLD MOVIE

あ な た が
気 づ け ば
マ ナ ー は
変 わ る 。

→ Would like to see how they diagram *The Bourne Ultimatum*.

BADH
Accounting

→ Royal E Skrewd Accounting is no longer in business.

Location → Tokyo, Japan
Credit → Johan Eklund

Location → Vancouver, Canada
Credit → Nina and Félix Houle

The sign reads:

BRUCE TRAIL
SIDE TRAIL
NIAGARA TO TOBERMORY

**OBESE
INDIVIDUAL'S
AGONY
Side Trail
200 m**

AN ALTERNATIVE LOOP TRAIL,
THROUGH A WONDERLAND OF ROCKS.
PART OF THE ESCARPMENT
BIOSPHERE CONSERVANCY.

→ Bit on the heavy side? You're going to love this hike.

Location → Wiarton, Canada
Credit → Mary Haller

→ Nice to see feminism is finally taking hold in Mexico.

Location → Chetumal, Mexico
Credit → Lisa McCallum

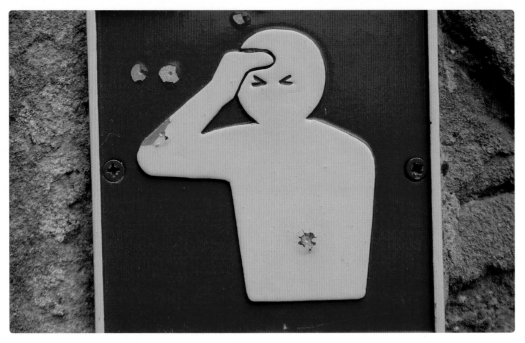

→ Caution: Migraine approaching.

Location → Wales
Credit → Andy Meyer

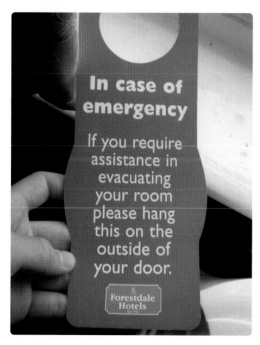

→ Honey, it's the fire alarm again. Can you hang this on the door and come back to bed?

Location → Bath, England
Credit   → Andy Meyer

→ When Edvard Munch visits the Dead Sea.

Location → Dead Sea, Jordan
Credit   → Karen Inda

→ Blind people are screwed.

Location   → A castle in Wales
Credit   → Andy Meyer

→ Spit in the urinal makes it difficult to enjoy the smell and look of splattered urine.

Location → Men's toilets (where else?), Rotorua, New Zealand
Credit → Barbara Roper

→ You can eat it, kayak on it, use it to treat inoperable cancer and stop Dutch Elm disease ... anything!

Location → Altoona, Pennsylvania, USA
Credit → Melissa Persun

→ Usually the best way to keep your shoes from getting stolen is to keep them on your feet.

Location → Dharamsala, India
Credit → Patricia Colley

No Paraphernalia

嚴禁擺放雜牛

→ Working hard to put an end to paraphernalia once and for all.

Location → Hong Kong
Credit → Paul Bolding

→ You wouldn't want to mess up the area around a squat toilet with an unclean foot.

Location → Hua Hin Beach Cafe, Thailand
Credit → Mark Pickup

→ Electric bills getting you down? What are you waiting for? Now's the time to switch to Porn and join millions of extremely satisfied customers.

Location → Koh Lanta, Thailand
Credit → Helena Edblad

→ What legalisation of drugs might look like.

Location   → Beijing, China
Credit   → Greg Earhart

→ New spa treatment? Get papered with our new fecal face therapy.

Location → San Francisco, California, USA
Credit → Regynn Lesser

→ Some people feel the need to announce it.

Location → Johannesburg, South Africa
Credit → Nelia Gunn

→ Motto: 'Our name says it all.'

Location   → Glenview, Illinois, USA
Credit   → Martin Dula

→ Making Ends Meet meets its end.

Location → Oakland, California, USA
Credit → Nicole Clausing

→ You might hurt their branches and/or feelings.

Location → Stockton, California, USA
Credit → Kaitlyn O'Rinn

FROM THE AUTHOR
Doug Lansky

→ I started photographing funny signs when, like many of you, I was caught off guard by a few signs during my travels. Now, 15 years later, I've received about 40,000 sign photos from travellers. And there are great new ones coming in every day. Thank you for continuing to send in signs, rate the signs others have submitted, and write your own funny captions for them at www.signspotting .com. So far, since launching the website in 2000, we've been able to give away an around-the-world ticket on the Star Alliance to the photographer of the best Signspotting photo of the year, as well as US$50 to each contributor in the Signspotting books – that's US$24,000 to date.

If you like the Signspotting books, you may also enjoy the following:

→ **THE SLIDESHOWS_**The Art of Miscommunication and The Secrets of Effective Miscommunication

After numerous requests, I've put together a funny slideshow of my favourites called 'The Art of Miscommunication' that highlights the cultural difference between what we say and what we mean. There's also a corporate version focused on the funniest failed marketing efforts called 'The Secrets of Effective Miscommunication'. While tens of thousands of consultants can tell companies how to market and brand their products the right way, this hilarious show focuses on how NOT to do it. These shows may be coming to a fine arts center, university, or business near you. For more information, see www.signspotting.com/events.

→ **THE EXHIBIT_**The Signspotting Project

Please keep your eyes open for The Signspotting Project – one of the funniest exhibits you'll ever see. We enlarged over 100 of the wackiest sign photos and mounted them back onto real metal signs at approximately life size and put them all on display in the centre of a city. At the global launch of the free exhibit in Stockholm, it became the biggest attraction in the city with 30,000 daily visitors. To see if any of these events are coming your way, check www.signspotting.com/events.

More sign photos please

There are so many great signs that have not yet been photographed, and with new signs going up every day, the only way to gather them is with an army of travellers. In other words, you. Please continue to send in your sign photos at www.signspotting.com.